Silk Flowers

1. Pull the center off of the flower petals.

2. Separate each of the flower layers.

3. Glue a bottle cap to the center of the flower.

Sweet Daughter

by Sherelle Christensen

Who can resist the beautiful flowers on this page? These wonderful embellishments are made by taking apart a silk flower and adding a bottle cap center. This page illustrates how bright colors can draw attention to a black and white photo.

Journaling on vellum allows you to make your statements without distracting from the main focal point.

MATERIALS:
Design Originals (3 Brass Bottle Caps; #0666 Girl Pink Sayings Stickers; #0585 Little Girls paper) • *Bazzill* Watermelon cardstock • Vellum • *ColorBox* Cat's Eye Chestnut Roan ink • Tag • Ribbon • Safety pin • 2 silk flowers • E6000 • Glue stick

INSTRUCTIONS:
Ink the edges of the Watermelon cardstock. Cover tag with Little Girls paper. Cut out your favorite images and glue them to the page with the photo. Print title and journaling on vellum. Add ribbons, safety pin, and title to the tag. Adhere the tag and journaling to the page. Remove the centers from 2 flowers. Glue flowers, caps and stickers in place.

Distressed Papers

1. Glue paper to cardstock backing and sand with medium weight sandpaper.
2. Apply acrylic paints to edges of paper with dry bristle brush, dragging color to create streaks.
3. Tear paper edges and apply chalks or chalk inks.
4. Apply chalk inks to edges to create aged look. Drag color across paper to create uneven streaks and blotches.
5. Crumple paper. Flatten and apply chalk inks lightly to surface. When dry, iron paper to flatten completely.
6. Apply sheer glazes to paper to tint.
7. Paint paper with coffee. Place on plastic sheet, and sprinkle with instant coffee crystals. Let dry.
8. Apply Magic Mesh to paper, and spray with colored paint. Remove Magic Mesh when dry.
9. Stamp paper with chunky stamps and inks or acrylics.

My Sister... Kelley

by Lisa Vollrath

Black and white can produce such dramatic art! Here is an inspiring example to create a clipboard frame. Magic Mesh, bottle caps, stickers, and ribbons really grab your attention and draw your eye right into the photo.

Linen design papers look so textured you want to reach out and touch them.

MATERIALS:
Design Originals (Black Bottle Caps; #0673 Typewriter ABCs stickers; Papers: #0709 Linen Large Floral, #0711 Linen Diamond, #0714 Linen Vine) • Large clipboard • 4" x 6" photo • 5" x 7" plexiglass sheet • *Magic Mesh* White Medium Weave • *Pebbles Inc.* Thoughts Twist Ties • Assorted ribbon • White Rub-On • *ColorBox* Lamp Black inkpad • Black acrylic paint • E6000 • Glue stick

INSTRUCTIONS:
Basecoat the clipboard with Black acrylic paint, dabbing on clip to texture. Let dry. • Tear the Linen Large Floral paper roughly to the shape of the clipboard. Edge with Lamp Black ink. Glue to clipboard. • Tear a strip of Linen Diamond paper 2³/₄" wide. Edge with Lamp Black ink. Glue across the lower section of the clipboard, wrapping to back. • Cut a piece of Magic Mesh the length of the clipboard. Pull several lengthwise threads to remove. Clip unravelled edge of mesh in irregular pattern. Position mesh on the left side of the board, trimming the edge as necessary. • Tear a rectangle of Linen Vine paper roughly the size of the plexiglass. Edge with Lamp Black ink. Position the Linen Vine piece, photo and plexiglass under the clip. Glue paper and photo in place if desired. • Apply Rub-On to the plexiglass. • Flatten Black bottle caps. Decorate with letter stickers, and glue to the Linen Diamond strip with E6000. Tie ribbons and twist ties to the back of the clip, trimming to desired length.

Add names, titles and dates to pages. Here the bottle caps are tied to a twill ribbon for added dimension.

Bottle Cap and Sticker Alphabets

Working with Wire

Bring a new dimension to your scrapbook pages with the addition of brilliantly colored wires. Use them for accents, titles, borders… your pages will be stunning!

22 gauge wire is flexible, works easily and holds its shape. It works well for Swirls, Shapes, letters/words, Jig designs and Twisted Coils.

24 gauge wire is flexible. It is best for Twisted Coils, and flattened Coils for alphabet letters, shapes or hair.

26 gauge wire is very flexible. It is great for wrapping, stitching and beading accents to your page.

Adhesives should be liquid and tacky. Suitable adhesives for wire to paper include Memory Mount, Perfect Paper Adhesive, Gem-Tac or E6000.

Round-nose pliers are perfect for twisting Swirls and Curves and for guiding wire into almost any shape.

Wire cutters make cutting wire easy. Cutters are available as a separate tool and some pliers include wire cutters.

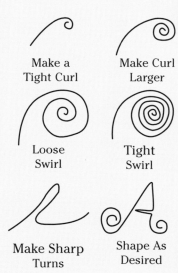

Make a Tight Curl

Make Curl Larger

Loose Swirl

Tight Swirl

Make Sharp Turns

Shape As Desired

Start by making a tight curl around the tip of Round-nose pliers. Attach this loop to a bottle cap. **Hint:** It is not necessary that items and letters be shaped exactly.

Use pliers and/or your fingers to shape more swirls and curves.

Tip: Use pliers as an aid to make sharp turns and to coax wire gently to the desired shape.

Hop Over Card
by Andrea Gibson

Hop right over and make this bunny card, or create a fun embellishment for a scrapbook page. This is a great beginner project for working with wire.

BUNNY JIG

BUNNY PATTERN

MATERIALS:
Design Originals 2 White Bottle Caps • *Bazzill* cardstock (Parakeet, Vanilla) • White ribbon • Small google eyes • *Artistic Wire* (Egg White 22 gauge, Wire jig) • *Making Memories* (Jersey UC foam stamps, Evolution Rub-On letters) • Pink Chalk • Decorative scissors • Square punch • Round-nose pliers • Wire cutters • White acrylic paint • Skewer • Sandpaper • Foam dots • *Therm O Web* Zots 3D

INSTRUCTIONS:
Prep: Flatten 2 caps. • Punch holes in the caps following the diagram. • Use sandpaper to distress each cap. Apply Pink chalk to the cheeks. • **Ears**: Cut 2 pieces of White wire 5" long. Shape the ears and feed the ends of the wires through the ear holes. Hot glue the wire ends to the back of the head cap. • **Whiskers**: Cut 2 White wires 6" long. Holding the wires together, poke the ends of the wire through the whisker holes from the back. Separate the wires. Curl each end around a skewer. • **Body**: Make White jump rings by coiling the wire around a skewer or paintbrush. Cut the coil into rings. Join the body to the head. Glue the eyes in place. • **Tail**: Cut a 4" piece of White wire. Shape the tail. Thread the wire ends to the back of the cap and hot glue in place. • **Card**: Cut Vanilla cardstock 6¾" x 7½". Fold in half to 3¾" x 6¾". Cut Parakeet cardstock 3⅝" x 6¾". Trim the bottom edge with decorative scissors. Adhere the Parakeet mat to the front of the card. Stamp the card with White paint. Let dry. Apply the Rub-On word to the card. • Punch a hole in the upper corner of the card front. Tie a ribbon through the hole. • **Finish**: Attach the rabbit to the card with foam dots.

MATERIALS:

Design Originals 6 Gold Bottle Caps • *Artistic Expressions* metal background page • *7gypsies* paper • Old lace • Rick-rack • Charm • Buttons • *L'il Davis* wooden flower • *Memory Lane* ribbon • *Plaid* acrylic paint (Cream, Brown, Pink) • Rust ink • Awl • Circle punches (1¼", ¾")

INSTRUCTIONS:

Background: Paint the metal background Cream. Let dry. Apply a thin coat of Brown paint and rub off while wet. Let dry. Dry brush with Pink. Let dry. • Tear corrugated paper larger than your photo. Ink the edges of the paper and the photo with Rust. Adhere cardboard and photo to metal background.•

Accents: Tear a scrap of script paper. Adhere 3 old buttons and glue in place. • Adhere lace and rick-rack to the bottom of the photo. Paint a wooden flower Pink. Let dry. Add a heart charm. • Write or computer print "favorite things" on script paper. Tear out the words and glue in place. Glue the wood flower in place. •

Bottle cap booklets: Flatten caps. Pierce each cap with an awl. Lay one cap on top of the other so the hole placement is consistent. Add rounds of punched cardstock, computer generated text and old lace. Pierce holes in the page and attach the cap booklets with ribbon.

My Favorite Things
by Carol Wingert

Reminiscent of the old stone fireplace, this embossed metal background has an irresistible texture. Lace and old buttons create a bit of nostalgia and focus your attention on this charming photograph.

Distressed Background

1. Paint metal tile Cream.

2. Paint Brown over the Cream.

3. Rub off the Brown while wet.

4. Dry brush with Pink.

Dedicate a scrapbook to all the times your daughters and their friends get dressed up, and you will have a treasure trove of memories to look back on.

UPPER LEFT DETAIL PATTERN

TOP LEFT JIG

TITLE PATTERN

Embellishments with Wire

MATERIALS:

Design Originals (5 Silver Bottle Caps; #0686 Princess Stickers) • *Bazzill* cardstock (White, Petunia, Romance) • *Artistic Wire* (Non Tarnish Silver 22 gauge, Writing system) • *Making Memories* Jersey UC foam stamps • White paint • Sheer Pink ribbon • Seed beads (White, Pink, Clear) • Pliers (Round-nose, Nylon jaw) • Wire cutters • Silver embossing powder • Embossing ink • Heat gun • Sandpaper • *Therm O Web* SuperTape • Glue stick

INSTRUCTIONS:

Background: Cut these strips: Romance 2½" x 12" and ¾" x 2½", Petunia 2¾" x 10". Glue in place. Emboss "Diva" with Silver. • **Photos:** Adhere the small photos to the Petunia strip. • Cut a Petunia mat ½" larger than the photo. Glue the mat and photo to the page. • Emboss the page corners with Silver. • **Accents:** Flatten all caps. Lightly paint the caps White. • Punch holes across from each other on 4 caps. • Shape the word "Diva" with Silver wire leaving 4" tails. Coil the ends into a filigree shape, adding beads as desired. Close the wire ends by making a loop with round-nose pliers. Flatten the coils and wire words with nylon jaw pliers. Attach to the layout with wires. • Make Silver jump rings by coiling wire and cutting the rings apart. Connect 3 caps together. Adhere to the page with SuperTape. • Apply stickers. Scuff stickers lightly with sandpaper. • **Dangles:** Punch 3 holes in the remaining cap. • Cut 3 wires 3" long. • Thread each wire into a hole. Bend the end around the cap edge to secure. Add beads as desired. Make a swirl at the end. • Adhere the cap to the page with SuperTape. • Wrap ribbon around page and adhere to back of page.

FLOWER DIAGRAM OF BOTTLE CAP

FLOWER PATTERN

Girls just wanna have fun! This page takes you back to those happy times with friends.

Girls Just Wanna Have Fun

by Andrea Gibson

MATERIALS:

Design Originals (4 Black Bottle Caps; #0670 Citrus Brights Stickers) • *Bazzill* cardstock (Raven, Petunia, White) • Black gingham paper • *Artistic Wire* Rose 24 gauge • *Dymo* Tape Embosser • *Tsukineko* StazOn Jet Black ink • *Stamping Station* Flower die-cut • Hematite beads • Alphabet stamps • Round-nose pliers • Wire cutters • *Creating Keepsakes* computer fonts (CBX, Kelly's pen) • *Therm O Web* SuperTape • Glue stick

INSTRUCTIONS:

Background: Cut 11½" strips: Petunia 3", Gingham ¾". Glue the strips in place. • **Photo**: Cut a Petunia mat ¼" larger than the photo. Ink the edges of the photo and mat. Adhere both to the page. • **Title**: Computer print the title. Cut out the words. Ink the edges. Mat as desired. Glue in place. • Adhere a 1¼" square of Petunia and the date tape. • **Accents**: Flatten 4 caps. Adhere the "in the Pink" sticker to 1 cap. Adhere the cap to the title with SuperTape. • **Flowers**: Punch holes in 3 caps every third space. • Cut 3 wires 16" long. Thread the wire through the holes adding beads as desired. Petals are 1" long. • Ink the die-cut flowers. Glue the flowers in place. • Attach the caps to the page with wire. • Apply stickers. • Stamp the letters "F", "U", "N".

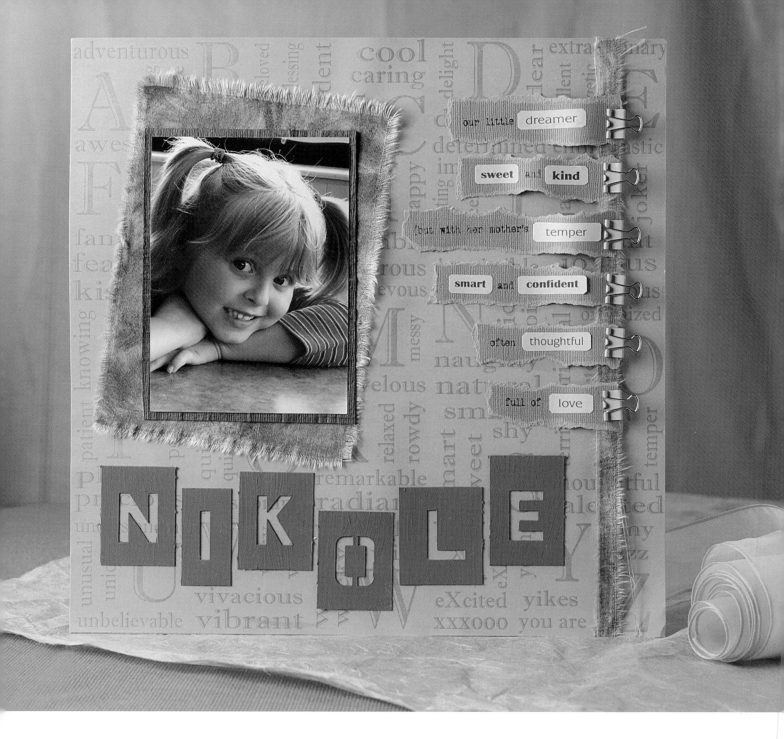

Clips and Clothespins

Little Notes about Nikole

by Lisa Vollrath

We are always looking for ways to spice up our borders. Give them a dimensional lift with Clips and Word stickers. You are really going to enjoy playing with these innovative embellishments.

The stickers allow you to emphasize phrases and the clips come in a variety of colors.

MATERIALS:

Design Originals (#0684 Pink A-Z Word Blocks paper; #1201 Pink Words stickers; #1902 Pink Clips) • *Bazzill* cardstock (Pansy, Heather) • Purple fabric scraps • 1" letter stencils • Purple acrylic paint • Adhesive

INSTRUCTIONS:

Paint the letter stencils Purple. Let dry. • Mat the photo with Pansy cardstock. • Tear a fabric scrap 1" larger than the mounted photo. Fringe the edges of the fabric by pulling threads. Glue photo to the fabric. • Tear a ½" x 15" long strip of fabric. Wrap the strip around the page as shown. Glue the ends to the back of the page. • Print journaling on Heather cardstock, leaving room for stickers where desired. Tear out lines of text and clip to the fabric with binder clips. • Adhere the photo and stencils on the page as shown.

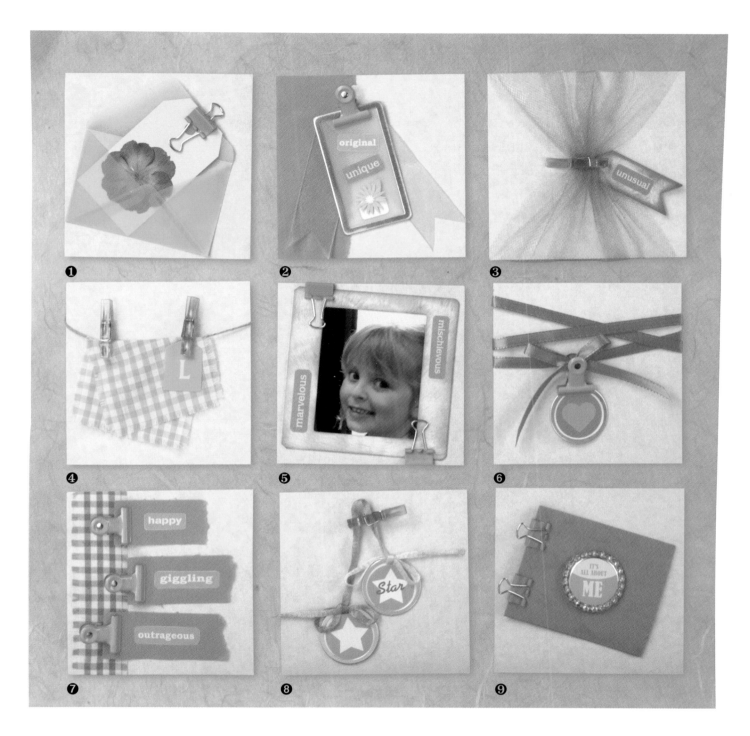

1. Clip decorated tags or ephemera to the flap of a vellum envelope.
2. Attach a spring clip to a page with a brad. Use it to hold a vellum tag decorated with word stickers and a scrap of ribbon.
3. Attach either tulle or ribbon to a page. Gather and clip with a mini clothespin. Tuck in a small tag.
4. Use mini clothespins to clip a small piece of fabric, letter stickers, or other embellishments to a hemp cord clothesline.
5. Mount a small photo in a slide mount. Decorate it with word stickers and use binder clips to attach it to the layout.
6. Wrap ribbon around a layout and thread it through the hole in a spring clip. Tie it in a bow. Clip tags, journaling or other embellishments to the ribbon.
7. Attach spring clips to a page with a brad. Clip strips of journaling and stickers to your layout.
8. Tie tags with ribbon, and clip them to a page with mini clothespins.
9. Clip several pages of journaling together with binder clips.

Pretty in Pink

Born to Be a Star
by Diana McMillan

Your photo is the most important aspect of your page design. On this page, the title bar and accent squares create a focal point for this beautiful image by simulating a frame that leads your eye into the photo. Soft pink bottle cap paper and stickers add the perfect background and accents.

MATERIALS:
Design Originals (4 Gold Bottle Caps; #0666 Girl Pink Sayings Stickers; #0678 Girl Pink paper) • 5" x 7" photo • *Bazzill* cardstock (Petunia, Romance) • Pink fiber • Glitter glue • *ColorBox* Cat's Eye ink (Orchid, Warm Violet, Quick Silver) • *Therm O Web* (Zots 3D, Memory Tape Runner)

INSTRUCTIONS:
Title: Computer print the title so it fits on 2" x 5" Romance cardstock and cut it out. Ink the edges with Silver, Violet, and Orchid. Wrap fibers around the bottom of the title. • **Cutting:** Cut a Petunia title mat 2½" x 7¾". Cut four 2" accent squares from Romance cardstock. • Cut a Romance photo mat 5¼" x 7¼". Cut a large Petunia photo mat 7¾" x 7¾". • Ink all the edges with Orchid, Violet, and Silver. • Adhere the title and a square to the Petunia mat with Zots 3D. • **Assembly**: Adhere Petunia mat to Girl Pink background paper. Adhere photo to small mat. Attach photo/mat and squares to the Petunia mat with Zots. • Adhere title and a square to the Petunia title mat. Attach title mat to the page with Memory Tape Runner. • **Caps**: Flatten 4 caps. Fill the trough with glitter glue. Let dry. • Apply stickers. Adhere caps to the squares with Zots 3D.

Soft Colors

Muted colors add a soft touch to any scrapbook page or card. You'll love using papers, stickers, fibers, ribbons and accents to add details to your creations.

These soft colors... on papers, stickers, bottle caps, clips and clothespins from Design Originals are perfect for baby pages and girly themes.

Extraordinary Love Card
by Sherelle Christensen

Create your own trinkets that state a personal message quickly and easily! Embellish metal tags with Design Originals stickers.

MATERIALS:
Design Originals (#0684 Pink A-Z Word Blocks paper; Stickers: #1201 Pink Words, #1205 Princess) • Lavender Plaid paper • *Kopp Design* metal tag • Ribbon • Adhesive

INSTRUCTIONS:
Cut a piece of the pink paper approximately 5" x 8". Fold in half to 4" x 5". • Cut a strip of Lavender Plaid 2" x 8". Adhere it to the outside of the card. Write "I love you" across each edge of the Plaid. • Tie ribbons to the long metal tag with a Lark's Head knot. Add stickers. Adhere to the card. • Apply stickers to the round metal tag. Staple a folded ribbon to the tag. Adhere tag to the card.

Sunshine Card
by Andrea Gibson

Add bottle caps to beaded wire for a new look on pages and cards.

MATERIALS:
Design Originals (1 Gold Bottle Cap; #0666 Girl Pink Sayings Stickers; #0988 Small White Mount; #0678 Girl Pink paper) • *Bazzill* Romance cardstock • *Artistic Wire* (Egg White 22 gauge; Wire beads: 4 Pink, 6 Natural) • *Ranger* Distress Walnut Stain ink • Sandpaper • *Therm O Web* SuperTape

INSTRUCTIONS:
Cut cardstock 4" x 12". Fold into thirds to 4" x 4". The card face is the middle part. One end will fold to the inside to hide the wires. Ink the edges. • Cut Girl Pink paper 3" x 3". Ink the edges. Ink the White mount. Adhere paper and mount to the front of the card. • Flatten the cap. Punch holes referring to photo. Add sticker and distress with sandpaper. • Cut 2 White wires 6" long. Thread wires under cap through holes across from each other. Add wire beads on each side of cap. Position wire/cap embellishment on card. Bend the wire ends to the back of card. Secure with SuperTape, trim wire as needed.

Sweet, Sweet Delanie
by Carol Wingert

You can't go wrong when you choose colors that match your photograph. Pink and blue fabric and stickers accent this page nicely. The buckle and bottle caps add dimension and texture.

MATERIALS:
Design Originals (4 Gold Bottle Caps; #0670 Citrus Brights Stickers) • 8½" x 8½" lightweight cardboard • *Junkitz* (Fabric, Buckle) • Organza fabric • Pink rick-rack • *Making Memories* flower brads • 1 small tag • *7gypsies* photo turns • Pink ink • *Golden* White gesso • Sewing machine • White thread • Foam dots

INSTRUCTIONS:
Background: Paint cardboard with White gesso. Let dry. • Sew fabric to the cardboard. • Fold the organza into pleats. Sew in place. Sew the rick-rack down the center of the organza. • Adhere photo in place. • **Accents**: Paint caps with White gesso. Let dry. • Apply stickers to the caps. • Lightly dry brush stickers with White gesso. • Adhere the caps to the ruffled organza background with foam dots. • Adhere the buckle to the fabric with flower brads. Attach the buckle to the right side of the page. • Write the title on the tag. Ink the tag edges with Pink. Attach a title tag to the buckle.

Fabric Accents

It's all about Texture! Textiles come in many forms... fabric, ribbon, trims, fibers. You can literally change the feel of a page with an interesting fabric.

Chenille adds softness, fur gives loft and warmth, velvet means elegance, and gingham will take you into a country farm house every time. Ribbons add color, text, and movement. You are going to love adding textiles.

MATERIALS:

Design Originals (#0687 Blue A-Z paper; #0682 Pink Tags ABCs stickers) • Cardstock (Pink, White) • Pink chenille fabric • Ribbon • Buttons • Pink silk flower • Pink Word twill • White flock • Markers (Black, Pink) • Sewing machine • Adhesive

INSTRUCTIONS:

Background: Cut the Blue A-Z paper to 11½" square. • **Title**: Cut a 6" square of Pink chenille and a 6" Light Teal ribbon. • Cut White cardstock 2½" x 3". Write the title with a Black marker, outlining the letters with Pink. • Tie ribbons to the Tag stickers. Arrange all the title elements on the Blue A-Z paper. Attach each element with a Zig Zag stitch. • Apply flock to the petals of a Pink flower. Glue the flower in place. Glue buttons to the center of the flower. • **Assembly**: Zig Zag stitch the Blue A-Z paper to a Pink 12" cardstock. • Adhere the photos to the page. • Cut out a White cardstock tag 2¼" x 4". Stitch around the border. Attach a chenille scrap to the hole in the tag. Write your journaling on the tag. Adhere the tag to the page. • Adhere the Pink Word twill to the bottom of the page.

Gracie's Doll

by Sherelle Christensen

This page is packed with wonderful texture ideas.

A scrap of chenille fabric makes the perfect title mat, while twill with printed words continues to be a favorite page enhancement. And here's a new way to use silk flowers. Check out the flocking on the petals! What a wonderful way to add a bit of sparkle to a layout.

A double layer of buttons provides that bit of added dimension without being too bulky.

1. Fray fabric edges by removing threads to create a soft feathery look.

2. Run the fabric through a Xyron machine to add adhesive to the back.

3. Press fabric to the shiny side of freezer paper to stiffen it.

Tips for Using Fabric

Ballerina Girl

by Sherelle Christensen

Whether your little princess is a dancer, cook, seamstress, or just loves to play with dolls, make a page themed just for her. "Princess" stickers give you so many ways to describe your "American beauty".

MATERIALS:
Design Originals (6 Silver Bottle Caps; #0686 Princess Stickers) • *Bazzill* cardstock (Wisteria, White) • Pink silk flower • Pink eyelet lace • Metal button • Silver embossed metal strip ¾" x 5" • Metal rim tag • Safety pin • Sheer Lavender ribbon • Pink chenille fabric 2¼" x 11" • Rubber stamps ("Lil' Ballerina", "dancer") • Ink (Pink, Lavender, White) • Pink acrylic paint • Hole punch • E6000 • Glue stick

INSTRUCTIONS:
Prep: Paint the Silver metal strip, metal rim tag, and button with Pink acrylic. Let dry. • Stamp the word "dancer" on Wisteria paper with White ink. Cut out and adhere to tag. • **Background:** Ink the edges of the photo with Pink. • Adhere photo and chenille to Wisteria paper. • Stamp "Lil Ballerina" on White with Pink and Lavender inks. Cut out and glue in place. • **Collage:** Tear White cardstock 4" x 5¼". Ink the edge with Pink. Glue in place. • Cut mats: Wisteria 2½" x 4", White 2½" x 3½". • Punch a hole in each end of the Wisteria mat. Add a ribbon on one side and pin the tag on the other side. Write title on the White mat. Ink the edges with Pink. Layer lace, metal strip, and mats. Glue in place. **Accents:** Adhere stickers to the caps. Glue caps, flower, and button in place with E6000. • Cut small strips of White and write descriptive phrases on them. Glue in place.

MATERIALS:

Design Originals (#0685 Pink A-Z paper; Stickers: #1201 Pink Words, #1205 Princess; 2 Silver Bottle Caps) • Chipboard • Ribbon • Pink iridescent sequins • Acrylic paint • Black marker • Sanding block • Adhesive

INSTRUCTIONS:

Flatten both bottle caps. • Sand around the edges of the paper and stickers for a distressed look. • Cut a chipboard photo mat 1" larger than the photo. Cut a chipboard tag for the title. Paint chipboard with acrylic paint. Let dry. Sand the edges. • Adhere the photo to the larger chipboard mat and staple folded ribbons in place. Apply sticker to a cap and adhere to the mat. Adhere the matted photo to the page. • Write the title on the title tag. Flatten a bottle cap and apply the sticker. Adhere it to the tag. Staple ribbons in place. • Add stickers and sequins around the photo. Write the journaling with a Black marker.

It's A Girl Thing
by Sherelle Christensen

Give your layout both line and movement when you create a dramatic border with Pink Words stickers. This "all girl" layout uses iridescent pink sequins to form the 'bullets' between the words.

Flattened silver bottle caps add that bit of sparkle that complements the gleam in this little girl's eyes.

Folded ribbons are stapled in place, adding a bit more metal, color, and texture.

Finally, have you thought of making a tag from heavy cardboard, matboard, or chipboard? It stands out just a bit more than the usual cardstock.

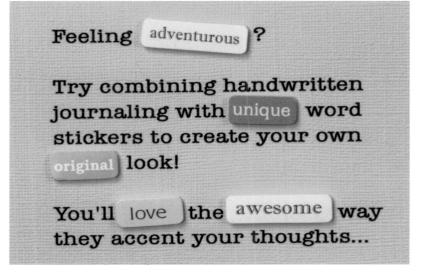

Accent with Words

You'll love adding little notes, frames, accents and details with tiny word stickers. Add them almost anywhere!

Daytona Beach
by Susan Keuter

Catch a wave on a sandy shore long after you come home. Vacation pages keep the memories alive.

MATERIALS:
Design Originals (2 Gold Bottle Caps; #0666 Girl Pink Sayings Stickers; #0590 Seashells paper) • *Bazzill* cardstock (Walnut, Dawn, White) • *Autumn Leaves* Date Rub-Ons • *May Arts* ribbon • White 1" wide rick-rack • *Making Memories* Alphabet Stamps • Brown ink • 1/8" hole punch • *JudiKins* Diamond Glaze • *Magic Scraps* Scrappy Glue

INSTRUCTIONS:
Background: Cut Pink cardstock 5½" x 11½". Cut Seashell paper 6" x 11½". Adhere to Brown cardstock as shown in photo. Glue the rick-rack over the seam. Stamp the title with Brown ink. • **Mat**: Cut a White mat ½" larger than the photo. Mount the photo to the mat. Apply Rub-On letters for name and/or date. Punch holes in photo edge and tie ribbons thru them. Adhere photo mat to page. • **Embellishments**: Flatten 2 caps. Punch a hole in each cap. Adhere stickers and cover with Glaze. Let dry for at least 24 hours. • Thread ribbons through the holes in the caps. Glue caps to the page.

Rachael
by Susan Charles

Tinted bottle caps dangle from wire to make a playful border while the pink stickers provide commentary. Pink mats complement the colors in the photo and the Runaway Doll paper.

MATERIALS:
Design Originals (3 Gold Bottle Caps; #0666 Girls Pink Sayings Stickers; Papers: #0500 TeaDye Keys, #0587 Runaway Doll) • *Artistic Wire* Maroon • Pink organza ribbon • Cardstock (Pink, Green) • Ink (*Ranger* Adirondack Raisin; *ColorBox* Cat's Eye Orchid) • 1/16" hole punch • *Therm O Web* (Zots 3D, Zots Large Dots, Memory Tape runner)

INSTRUCTIONS:
Tear and ink Keys paper. Glue to page. • Flatten caps. Punch holes. Tint with Raisin ink. Attach organza bows with wire. Adhere to page. • Mat photos with Pink and Green. Adhere to page.

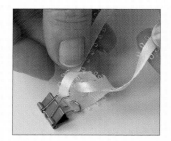

Overhand Knot

Lark's Head Knot

Simple Knots

Easy Bow

Bunny Ear Bow
Form 2 ears with two loops from one ribbon.

Make an Overhand knot with the "ears". Pull them taut to form a bow.

MATERIALS:
Design Originals 1 Gold Bottle Cap • *Basic Grey* paper • *Junkitz* button • *7gypsies* index tab • *Bazzill* (Juneberry cardstock, mini brads) • *Memory Lane* ribbon • *Ma Vinci's* Reliquary stamp • *Ranger* Pink ink • *Plaid* Pink acrylic paint • Folder by Carol Wingert • Silk flower • 1" circle punch • Craft knife • Sandpaper • E6000

INSTRUCTIONS:
Background: Cut an 8½" x 8½" piece of Juneberry cardstock. Punch 7 paper circles. Fold the circles in half and glue them to the right edge of the background. • Cut a ⅝" x 8½" piece of stripe paper. Glue it to the left side of the background. Add brads. •
Folder: Cut a stripe cardstock sheet 7¾" x 12". Trim one edge to a tab shape. Fold the cardstock in half. Ink the inside with Pink. Computer print the journaling and cut out the words in strips. Glue the strips inside the folder. Cut out 5 squares from the striped paper. Glue the squares inside the folder. • Sand the striped paper on the front of the folder. • Cut 3 small slits in the fold. Thread ribbons through the slits and wrap the left side of the folder. Tie ribbon ends in a bow on the front. • Adhere the photo over the ribbons on the inside. • Adhere photo over 2 of the ribbons and under 1 ribbon on the cover. • Stamp the date at the top. • Attach the index tab to the top of the folder. • **Flower center**: Layer silk petals on top of each other and glue together. Paint a cap with acrylic paint. Let dry. Glue a clear button on the cap. Glue cap to the center of the flower with E6000. • **Finish**: Glue the folder to the background. Glue the flower in place.

Princess Diaries
by Carol Wingert

Add fun and interest to a page by giving the viewer something to do. On this layout, a tab folder turns the page to show journaling.

MATERIALS:

Design Originals (4 Silver Bottle Caps; #0665 Boy Blue Sayings Stickers; Papers: #0583 Stories for Boys, #0582 Toys for Boys) • *Bazzill* Stonewash cardstock • Paper (Manila, Blue/Gray) • Plastic letters • *ColorBox* Cat's Eye ink (Amber Clay, Blue) • Black marker • Blue acrylic paint • E6000 • Glue stick

INSTRUCTIONS:

Background: Tear the Little Boys and Toys for Boys papers. Ink the edges with Amber Clay. Glue to cardstock. • Mat photo on Blue/Gray paper and adhere to page. **Title**: Paint the letters Blue. Let dry. Write "100% pure" with a Black marker on Manila paper. Tear a piece of Stories for Boys paper and adhere it to the title. Ink the edges with Blue. • Glue the letters to the title box. Adhere it to the page. • **Accents**: Flatten 4 caps. Adhere stickers to the caps. Glue caps to the page with E6000. • Cut small strips of Blue/Gray paper and write descriptions that fit your photo. Glue them in place.

100% Boy
by Sherelle Christensen

Here's a smile that will light up your life. Make a scrapbook page equally charming with easy accents and bottle caps.

Keepsake Box

Store little mementos in this keepsake box...the napkin from the baby shower, the hospital bracelet, his first pair of slippers, or use this as a photo box. The decorations are "all boy".

MATERIALS:

Design Originals (8 Gold Bottle Caps; #0665 Boy Blue Sayings Stickers; Papers: #0667 Boy Blue, #0582 Toys for Boys) • Cardboard school supply box • Blue ribbons • Large Tag • *Plaid* Mod Podge • Acrylic paint • E6000

INSTRUCTIONS:

Box: Cover the box with Boy Blue and Toys for Boys paper using Mod Podge. Paint any edges not covered by the paper. Let dry. Add another coat of Mod Podge and adhere the ribbon to the lid. • **Tag**: Cover the tag with Toys for Boys paper. Write the title with a Black marker. Add the ribbon. Adhere the tag to the box with Mod Podge. • **Accents**: Adhere stickers inside the caps. Glue caps to the box with E6000.

Boys Photo Frame

by Gail Ellspermann

Cuddles, dreams, hugs, bottle caps, beads and laughter... honor the gentle side of boys with this soft blue frame.

MATERIALS:

Design Originals (Bottle Caps: 7 Aqua, 7 Gold; #0665 Boy Blue Sayings Stickers; #0677 Boy Blue paper) • Wooden frame • Blue ribbon with White dots • Blue wire • Letter beads (Blue, Lavender) • Blue paint • Rubber stamps • *Tsukineko* Staz-On ink (Silver, Blue) • *Krylon* White spray paint • Matboard to fit frame • Small nails • Hammer • Photo mounts • Red Liner tape

INSTRUCTIONS:

Paint the frame Blue. Let dry. • Stamp the frame. • Flatten the Aqua caps. Paint the Gold caps White. Let dry. • Position and nail caps to the frame. Apply stickers to caps. Beginning at top left, anchor wire under bottle cap. Add letter beads to form a word. Wrap wire once around nail under cap, add letter beads, and wrap around next nail. Continue around the frame. • Apply Red Liner tape to the edge of frame. Add ribbon over the tape. • Cover matboard with Boy paper and nail in place. • Use photo corners to mount photo in place.

Bottle Cap Accents

Create clever tabs for the ends of a title or name with folded bottle caps.

Flatten a bottle cap then use two pair of pliers to fold it in half with the color on the outside. Wrap the cap around the ends of a cardstock strip then tighten. Glue the bottle caps and the cardstock strip to the page.

MATERIALS:
Design Originals (7 Silver Bottle Caps; #0675 Blue Alphabet Stickers; #0677 Boy Blue paper) • *Bazzill* cardstock (Jacaranda, Red, Sapphire) • *ColorBox* Cat's Eye ink (Cerulean, Scarlet) • 2 Blue mini brads • Deckle edge ruler • *Therm O Web* (Memory Tape Runner, Zots 3D)

INSTRUCTIONS:
Background: Cut a Sapphire strip 6" wide. Adhere it to the Boy Blue paper. • Tear a Jacaranda strip 4½" wide. Ink the edges. Adhere to page. • **Title**: Flatten caps. Adhere the stickers. Attach the caps to the page with Zots 3D. • **Photo**: Tear a Red mat 1" larger than the photo. Ink the edges. Adhere mat and photo to the page. • **Journaling**: Print the journaling on Red cardstock. Cut it out in a strip. Tear the bottom edge. Adhere the journaling paper to the page with mini brads.

Little Tyler sits in the middle of the floor laughing and smiling, playing with all of his favorite toys and all dressed up like a little cowboy wearing his favorite cowboy hat.

Giddy Up
by Diana McMillan

Ride 'em Cowboy! This charming photo draws you in and makes you smile. Simple layout design keeps the focus on your photo.

Title, how do I make thee?
Let me count the ways!
I can apply stickers to a bottle cap,
Or I can clip this tag to that.
Are clothespins just right for me?
Or shall I tag the letter "C"?
Ribbons, fibers, layered stuff,
Deciding what to use is tough.

Terrific Titles

Enjoy experimenting with all the fun combinations possible for adding excitement to your titles.

MATERIALS:
Design Originals (13 Silver Bottle Caps; Stickers: #0674 Red Alphabet, #0675 Blue Alphabet; Papers: #0583 Stories for Boys, #0585 Little Girls) • *Bazzill* cardstock (Light Blue, White, Cardinal, Blue Jay, Vanilla) • *ColorBox* Cat's Eye ink (Cerulean, Dune) • Star nailheads (small, large) • *Therm O Web* (Zots 3D, Memory Tape Runner)

INSTRUCTIONS:
Background: Tear 'Little Girls' and 'Stories for Boys' papers on the diagonal. Ink the edges. Adhere both papers to 12" x 12" White cardstock. • **Journaling**: Print words on Light Blue paper. Double-mat with Blue Jay and Cardinal cardstocks. Add small stars to the corners. Adhere the journaling box to the page. • **Photo**: Cut a Light Blue mat for the photo ¼" larger than the photo. Adhere the photo to the mat. Piece a Cardinal and Blue Jay mat 1" larger than the photo mat. Adhere the photo mat to the pieced mat. Add large stars. Adhere to the page. • Flatten caps. Add stickers. Adhere the caps to the page with Zots 3D.

All Girl, All Boy
by Diana McMillan

Metal embellishments add weight to the design of a page. In "All Boy, All Girl", the bottle caps support the title, counterbalance the light paper, and match the metal in the stars, creating unity in the design.

MATERIALS:

Design Originals (Bottle Caps: 2 Red, 4 Navy Blue; #1210 Patriotic Stickers) • *Bazzill* cardstock (White, Red, Periwinkle) • *Doodlebug* decorative paper • Transparency sheet • *Memories in the Making* Sticker Letters • *Making Memories* ("Rummage" Alphabet Stamps; White paint) • White acrylic paint • *Plaid* Mod Podge • *Magic Scraps* Scrappy Glue • Foam dots

INSTRUCTIONS:

Title: Paint the transparency with White paint. Let dry. • Hammer 2 Blue caps completely flat. Fold the caps over the edge of a counter top to crease each cap in half. Position the folded caps at the edges of the transparency title. Lightly tap the caps with a hammer to secure. Adhere sticker letters to the painted transparency. • **Mats:** Cut a Stripe mat 11½" x 11½". Glue Stripe mat to the White background. • Cut a White mat 8½" x 9⅜". Glue mat in place. • Cut a Red and Periwinkle mat 4½" x 6½". Mount photographs. Glue mats in place. • Stamp additional journaling.
• **Embellishments:** Adhere stickers to the caps. Cover the entire cap with a thin layer of Mod Podge. Let dry. • Attach caps with foam dots.

Snowcones
by Susan Keuter

Good photos always make attractive pages. These close-ups really do tell a story of a thousand words.

American Pride Pin
by Sherelle Christensen

Next time you need that "special touch" added to a patriotic scrapbook page, card, or gift, make this snappy ribbon embellishment. It's also great to wear pinned to your shirt! While you're at it, make three or four - all your friends and family will want one!

MATERIALS:

Design Originals (Bottle Caps: Red, Navy Blue; #1210 Patriotic Stickers) • Ribbon (wide Red, skinny Blue check) • Star shaped buttons

INSTRUCTIONS:

Cut Red ribbon to desired size. Fold as shown and staple. • Add pin to the back. • Add Blue checked ribbon. • Flatten the caps. Add stickers. Add star shaped buttons.

Patriotic Bottle Caps Flag

1. Punch holes in the bottle cap.

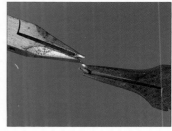

2. Open jump rings with pliers.

3. Connect caps together with jump rings.

Flag Day
by Diana McMillan

Stars and Stripes! It's Flag Day. Make a dramatic accent with patriotic stickers and bottle caps to honor the red, white and blue. This page is full of American spirit.

MATERIALS:
Design Originals (Bottle Caps: 8 Red, 4 Navy Blue; #1210 Patriotic Stickers; #0556 Word Tags Transparency; #0676 All American paper) • *Bazzill* cardstock (Blue, Red) • *WordsWorth* Freedom sticker • *ColorBox* Cat's Eye Cerulean ink • Silver stars • 17 jump rings • 2 pair pliers • *JudiKins* Diamond Glaze • *Therm O Web* (Memory Tape Runner, Zots 3D)

INSTRUCTIONS:
Background: Ink the edges of the Blue cardstock with Cerulean. • Cut a strip of All American paper 3¾" wide. Adhere to the page. • Adhere the Freedom sticker to the page. • **Photo**: Cut a Red mat 5½" x 8½". Tear the bottom edge. Add the stars. Attach the transparency with Glaze. Adhere the photo and mat to the page. • **Accents**: Flatten the caps. • Punch holes in bottle caps. • Join the caps together with jump rings. • Add the stickers. • Adhere the caps to the page with Zots 3D.

FREEDOM
by Wendy Silva

So many lives torn apart by our belief
and desire to live in a land that is free.
Men and women of all walks of life
fought to give us choice and liberty.

Such a generous and unselfish gift of life,
they sacrificed everything for others.
Because of their example of bravery and love,
we come together a nation, united as brothers.

Proud to be Americans, grateful for those
who have fought for what they believed.
And speechless for such a blessing of
freedom that together we have achieved.

A mighty flag is the symbol of American
freedom, one we proudly display.
The call of war we will answer, but peace
is what we wish for, what we hope and pray.

Ashley

by Diana McMillan

Give your project extra appeal! Tearing a side "v" in the surface paper adds shape, line, and texture to the design of this page, and keeps it from looking like the usual "square" layout.

MATERIALS:

Design Originals (Bottle Caps: 4 Red, 1 Yellow, 1 Navy Blue, 1 Green; Stickers: #0675 Blue Alphabet, #0664 School Days; #0676 All American paper) • *Bazzill* cardstock (Gold, Typhoon, Red, Ultra Blue) • *Therm O Web* (Memory Tape Runner, Zots 3D)

INSTRUCTIONS:

Background: Tear a "V" shape out of the Typhoon cardstock. Curl the edges back. Adhere to the All American paper with Memory Tape Runner. • Apply stickers to some of the caps on the All American paper. • **Photo**: Cut a Red mat ¼" larger than the photo. Adhere the photo to the mat. Cut an Ultra Blue mat ½" larger than the photo. Adhere the photo to the mat. Cut a Gold mat 1" larger. Adhere the photo and mat to the page. • **Journaling**: Print words on Gold cardstock. Cut out and adhere to the page. • **Accents**: Flatten the caps. Apply the stickers. Adhere the caps to the page with Zots 3D.

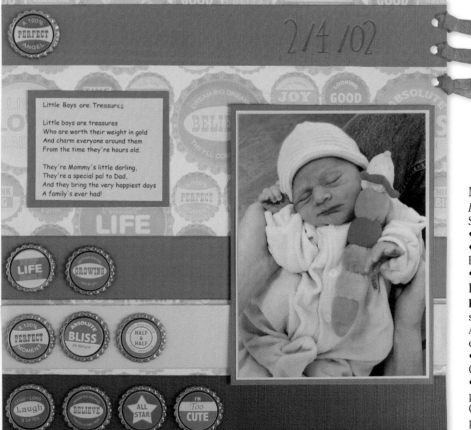

Perfect Baby

by Diana McMillan

Color and balance work well together on this "Perfect Baby" page. Your eye moves easily around the page because the elements are not crowded together. The colors in the stuffed animal inspired the striped background.

MATERIALS:

Design Originals (10 Silver Bottle Caps; #0664 School Days Stickers; #0676 All American paper) • *Bazzill* cardstock (Lava, Cantaloupe, Ivy, Blue) • *ColorBox* Cat's Eye ink (Cerulean, Scarlet, Evergreen, Amber Satin) • Blue number Rub-Ons • *Therm O Web* (Memory Tape Runner, Zots)

INSTRUCTIONS:

Background: Cut a 1¾" x 12" strip of each cardstock. Ink the edges. Adhere strips to the All American paper. • Add the date Rub-Ons. Flatten caps. Add stickers. Adhere to the page with Zots. • **Journaling**: Print words on Cantaloupe paper. Cut out and mat with Lava. Adhere to the page. • **Photo**: Cut a Cantaloupe mat ¼" larger than the photo. Cut a Lava mat ¼" larger than the Cantaloupe mat. Adhere mats and photo to the page.

Sunshine
by Andrea Gibson

When your photo says "Sunshine", make the perfect accent for your title with a bottle cap and wire. Express other personality traits with stickers on a linked bottle cap chain.

MATERIALS:
Design Originals (Bottle Caps: 5 Gold, 1 Yellow; #0664 School Days Stickers) • *Bazzill* cardstock (Crimson, Lemonade, Parakeet, Blue) • *Artistic Wire* 22 gauge (Lemon, Brown) • *Ranger* Distress Walnut Stain ink • *Making Memories* Philadelphia LC foam stamps • Copper embossing powder • Embossing ink pad • Heat gun • Round-nose pliers • Wire cutters • Pencil • *Therm O Web* SuperTape • Glue stick

INSTRUCTIONS:
Background: Cut these strips: Blue 3¼" x 11¾", Lemonade 3¾" x 8¾". Ink the edges. Glue in place. Stamp "Sunshine" on the Lemonade paper. • **Photos:** Cut Parakeet mats ¼" larger than the photos. Ink the edges. Glue mats and photos to the page. **Accents**: Flatten all caps. Cut a tag from Lemonade cardstock. Ink the edges. Stamp the name. Glue the tag in place. Punch holes in a cap and attach it to the tag with wire. Add the sticker.

SUN JIG

Sun: Punch holes around the Yellow cap in every other space. • Cut 5 pieces of each wire 7" long. Holding one wire of each color together, thread in a hole, across the back and out a hole on the other side. Use the round-nose pliers to make a loop in the end of each wire. • Continue for all wires. • Bend a zig zag in each sunray. • Heat emboss the cap with Copper. • Use small wires to attach the sun to the page. • **Bottle Cap Row**: Punch 1 hole on each end cap. Punch 2 holes in the middle caps, across from each other. • Coil Brown wire around a pencil and cut the coils apart to form jump rings. Attach the cap row together as in the photo. • Adhere the caps to the page with SuperTape.

SUN PATTERN

Wire Sunburst

Sisters

by Sherelle Christensen

Celebrate the sister you treasure with this touching expression of love.

MATERIALS:
Design Originals (6 Silver Bottle Caps; #0669 Vintage Children Stickers; #0679 Vintage paper) • Cardstock (Red, Tan) • Red ink • Ribbon • Silk flower • Vintage button • Square ring • Markers (Black, Red) • Staples • Sewing machine • Glue stick

INSTRUCTIONS:
Ink the edges of the Vintage paper with Red. • Mat 1 photo and the title on Red. Glue photo mat to page. • Sew second photo to the page. • Apply stickers inside 5 caps. Glue a small flower and a button into the last cap. Adhere ribbons and caps to page. Staple ribbon embellishment in place on title mat. • Adhere the title to the page.

Bottle Caps

Punch holes on opposite sides of bottle cap rim, and stitch to ribbon or fabric.

Punch a hole in the cap rim and use a safety pin to attach. Hang a charm from the pin before closing.

Create with Bottle Caps

1. Cut a circle of patterned paper, edge with ink, and glue it to a juice lid. Edge sticker with the same ink, stick it to a flattened bottle cap, and glue it inside the rim of a juice lid.

2. Flatten bottle cap and apply a sticker. Glue over ribbon loops, bow, or a flat piece of twill tape.

3 Apply a vintage image to a flattened bottle cap, then create a clear dome. Just apply a couple of Zots Clear Adhesive 3-D Dots to the image, then dip in Ultra Thick Embossing Enamel (UTEE). Heat with a heat gun until a clear, rounded shape melts in. Apply extra UTEE if desired.

4. Stitch colored or metallic threads through the buttonholes. Glue 1 layer of a small silk flower and a small button into a cap. Looks great with a skeletal leaf and a few strands of raffia.

5. Bottle caps look great when mixed with other embellishments. Try gluing them to the edge of a mount, or combining with binder clips.

6. Flatten a bottle cap, punch a hole in the rim with a 1/16" hole punch or nail, and hang from a jump ring. Rings can be threaded onto ribbon, pearl cotton, fibers, or through loosely woven fabrics or twill tape.

7. Use bottle caps as tags! Just punch a hole in the rim and thread a few strands of fibers or rayon floss through. These look great slipped into clear or vellum envelopes.

8. Punch holes on opposite sides of the cap rim, and thread onto ribbon, floss or fibers. 9. Tuck a cap into wrapped ribbons or fibers.

9. Tuck a cap into wrapped ribbons or fibers.

Bottle Cap Accents

Farm Life
by Shari Carroll

Give your page a rustic look to complement the topic by painting bottle caps. Make your own stickers with a 1" circle punch.

MATERIALS:
Design Originals (4 Gold Bottle Caps; #0542 Father's Farm paper) • *Bazzill* cardstock (Paper Bag, Root Beer) • *Cloud 9* Decorative papers • 1" Circle punch • Transparency film • *Hero Arts* Alphabet stamps • Black ink • Metal rusting kit • *Therm O Web* Zots • Glue stick • Ribbon

INSTRUCTIONS:
Background: Tear 1¾" strip of Paper Bag cardstock. Layer between 2 Cloud 9 papers. • **Photo**: Cut out the photo and layer as shown in the picture. Glue the photo to the page. • Trim the background to 8" x 10½". Adhere the background to the Root Beer cardstock. • **Journaling**: Print the journaling on the transparency. Sew the transparency to the page. • **Accents**: Flatten 4 caps. Rust the bottle caps following manufacturer's directions. • Punch four 1" circles from Father's Farm paper. Stamp "F", "A", "R", "M" in Black. Adhere the circles to the painted caps with Zots. • Adhere the caps to the transparency with Zots.

Western
by Carrie Edelmann Avery

This is a great example of letting the paper do the work for you. This layout is made with one background paper, one die-cut frame, stickers and metal embellishments.

MATERIALS:
Design Originals (5 Silver Bottle Caps; #0667 Walnut Numbers Stickers) • *EK Success* Letter stickers • *Heidi Grace* Copper piece • *Making Memories* brads • *Paper Loft* Western Paper • 4 Black eyelets • *My Mind's Eye* die cut frame • Stylus tool • *Tsukineko* StazOn Black ink or *Sharpie* marker• Eyelet tools • Glue dots • Fibers

INSTRUCTIONS:
Background: Mat photo with die-cut frame. Adhere to page. • **Accents**: Flatten caps. Adhere stickers. Glue in place. • Add brads between caps. • **Title**: Place Copper on a mouse pad. Write text on Copper using a ball point pen or stylus. Rub StazOn or a Sharpie marker onto Copper and immediately buff off. Add more ink into lines of the letters as desired. Attach Copper to the page with eyelets. Arrange alphabet stickers. • Tie fibers in knot and adhere ends to back of page.

Christmas Card

Use the title box alone to create a beautiful holiday card. Add a bottle cap, a sticker, a tiny bear, fabric, a flower and ribbon to give dimension.

Holiday Cheer

Combine soft holiday colors and images to create handmade cards for Christmas. These vintage style papers work well together... music, holly and Santa are fun symbols of the holidays.

Santa Card

Santa brings cheer to any holiday celebration. Choose bottle caps and stickers to highlight the front of this cheerful card.

Accordion Book

The accordion book album, in the lower right-hand corner of the scrapbook page, would make a lovely gift all on its own.

Decorate several pages with photos, journaling, ribbons and paper accents for a wonderful memento.

Wire Snowflake

Snowflake
by Andrea Gibson

Every snowflake is unique. Make a lovely snowflake accent with your own filigree design.

MATERIALS:
Design Originals 1 Gold Bottle Cap • *Artistic Wire* Egg White 22 gauge • White paint • Round-nose pliers • Wire cutters • Skewer • *Suze Weinberg* UTEE • Heat gun

INSTRUCTIONS:
Flatten a cap. Paint the cap White. Let dry. • Add a sticker. Sprinkle the sticker with UTEE. Heat and let cool .Punch holes in the cap following the diagram. • Cut 5 wires 6" long. Thread a wire through the cap, across the back and out a hole on the other side, leaving the same length tails on each end. Curl each end into a fil-igree shape. Repeat for remaining wires.

SNOWFLAKE JIG

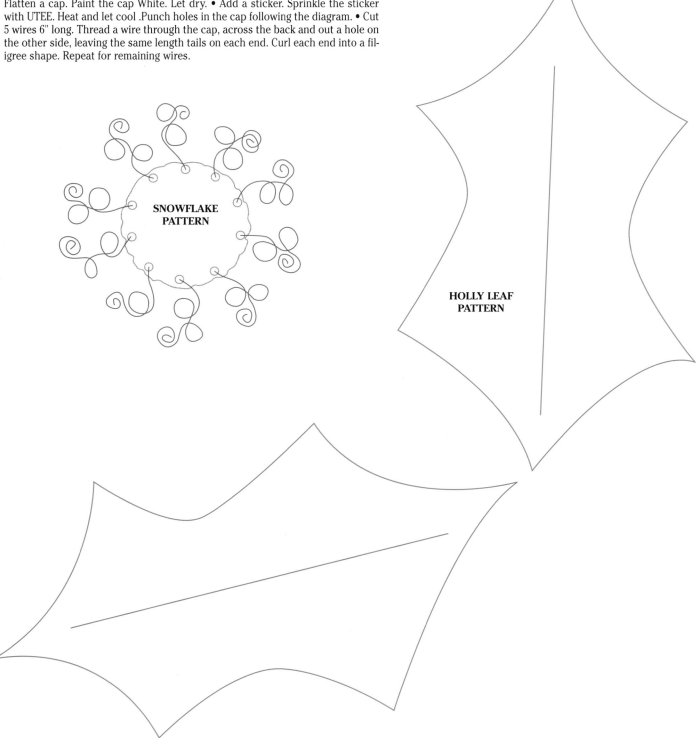

SNOWFLAKE PATTERN

HOLLY LEAF PATTERN

MATERIALS:
Design Originals (6 Red Bottle Caps; #0671 Holiday Sayings Stickers; #0478 Green Linen paper) • *Bazzill* Red cardstock • *ColorBox* Cat's Eye ink (Evergreen, Chestnut Roan) • *Therm O Web* (Memory Tape Runner, Zots 3D)

INSTRUCTIONS:
Accents: Cut 4 holly leaf shapes from Green Linen paper. Fold each leaf down the middle and run the fold across the Evergreen ink pad. Ink the edges of each leaf. • Apply stickers to caps. • Adhere leaves and caps to the page. • Cut a Red circle a little larger than the snowflake accent (see page 36). Adhere the Red circle and snowflake to the page. **Photo**: Cut a Red mat ½" larger than the photo. Tear the bottom edge. Ink the edge with Chestnut Roan. Adhere the photo and mat to the page.

Noel Joy
by Diana McMillan

Bottle caps with stickers make great seasonal accents. Here, the caps become holly berries and a snowflake.

These easy embellishments are inexpensive to make, and they make great stocking stuffers and gifts for your scrapbooking friends.

MATERIALS:

Design Originals (5 Black Bottle Caps; Stickers: #0673 Typewriter Alphabet, #0671 Holiday Sayings; #0988 Small White Mount) • *Bazzill* cardstock (Raven, Orange, Pear, White) • *Artistic Wire* Black 22-24 gauge • *Tsukineko* StazOn Jet Black ink • *ColorBox* Fluid Chalk Lime Pastel ink • Black ¾" wide rick-rack • Green bugle beads • 2 pair google eyes • Pliers • Wire cutters • Skewer • *Therm O Web* (SuperTape, Zots) • *Xyron* adhesive

INSTRUCTIONS:

Background: Trim Orange cardstock to 11¾" x 11¾". Adhere it to the Raven cardstock. • Cut 2 pieces of Pear cardstock 1⅞" x 5½". Tear an end. Ink the edges with Black. Cut 5" piece of rick-rack and fold in half. Staple it to a corner of one of the Pear rectangles. Adhere to the page as in the photo. • **Photos**: Ink the mount. Attach a photo to the back of the mount. Adhere the mount to the page. • Cut White mats ¼" larger than the photos. Ink the edges Black. Adhere mats and photos to the page. • **Accents**: Cut 11" of Black rick-rack for the spider and adhere it to the page. • Flatten the caps. • **Spider**: Punch holes according to the diagram. Press the cap into the Green ink pad. Let dry. • Cut four 24 gauge wires 6" long. Thread a wire in a hole and out a hole on opposite side.. Zig zag the legs and add a Green bead. Coil the end into a loop. Repeat for the remaining wires. • Adhere eyes with Zots. Attach the spider to the page with SuperTape. • **Boo**: Form the letter "B" with 22 gauge wire using the pattern. Attach to the page with wire. Apply stickers to 2 caps. Adhere the caps to the page with SuperTape. • **Cat**: Use the diagram to punch holes in 2 caps. • Using 22 gauge wire, cut 3 pieces 6" long for whiskers and tail. Cut 2 pieces 3" long for ears. • Thread 2 whisker wires by holding wires together. Poke the ends of wire through whisker holes from the back. Separate wires, coil each end around a skewer and form into whiskers. • Bend the other 6" wire in half. Shape the tail. Thread the ends through the tail holes. Secure the ends to the back of the cap with SuperTape. • Bend each 3" wire in half. Thread the ends into the ear holes. Shape the ears. Secure the ends to the back of the cap with SuperTape. • Attach the head to the body with wire. • Adhere the cat to the page with 24 gauge wire.

Note: To make rick-rack easier to attach, run it through a Xyron machine first.

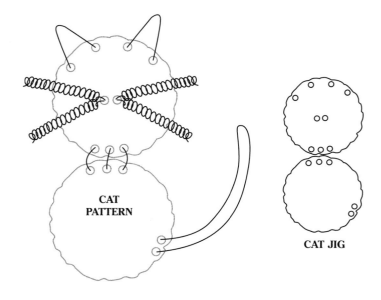

CAT PATTERN

CAT JIG

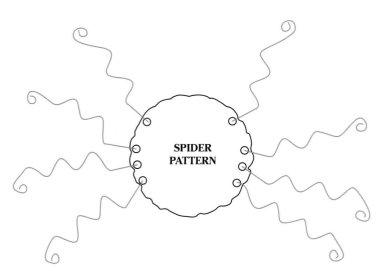

SPIDER PATTERN

SPIDER JIG

Boo
by Andrea Gibson

Black cats and spiders will help you scare up some Halloween memories with this fun layout.

Wire Cat, Spider & Boo with Bottle Caps and Wire

Spooky
by Sherelle Christensen

Those who find Halloween a "treat" are going to have a bewitching time making this boo-tiful album. Using a purchased book lets you get started on the fun right away.

Halloween papers, orange bottle caps and stickers make it easy to coordinate your themed elements. This is a great collage.

MATERIALS:
Design Originals (2 Orange Bottle Caps; #0671 Holiday Sayings Stickers; Papers: #0574 Pumpkins, #0575 Trick or Treat, #0576 Halloween Postcards) • *Bazzill* (Mini Book, Kraft cardstock) • Large tag • Orange ribbon • Lace • *ColorBox* Cat's Eye Chestnut Roan ink • Markers (Black, Orange) • Sandpaper • E6000 • Glue stick

INSTRUCTIONS:
Adhere Pumpkin paper to the front of the book. • Sand and ink edges. Cover a tag with Trick or Treat paper. Ink the edges. Add a ribbon. Glue in place. • Cut out images from Halloween Postcards and glue in place. Cut Kraft cardstock and write titles or journaling with a marker. • Adhere stickers to caps and adhere to the book with E6000.

Thank You Card
by Sherelle Christensen

Always say "thank you". That's what Mother taught us. This pretty card says it all with simple style. Frame your sentiment with color-coordinated buttons.

MATERIALS:
Design Originals #0688 Lime A-Z Word Blocks paper • White cardstock • Black marker • Green colored pencil • Assorted buttons • Glue dots

INSTRUCTIONS:
Cut a piece of Lime paper 5" x 7½". Fold in half to 3¾". • Write the title on a small piece of White cardstock with a Black marker. Highlight the letters with a Green colored pencil. Adhere to the center of the card. • Adhere various buttons around the title. • Write "thank you" around the outside of the buttons.

Wire Bat and Pumpkin with Bottle Caps and Wire

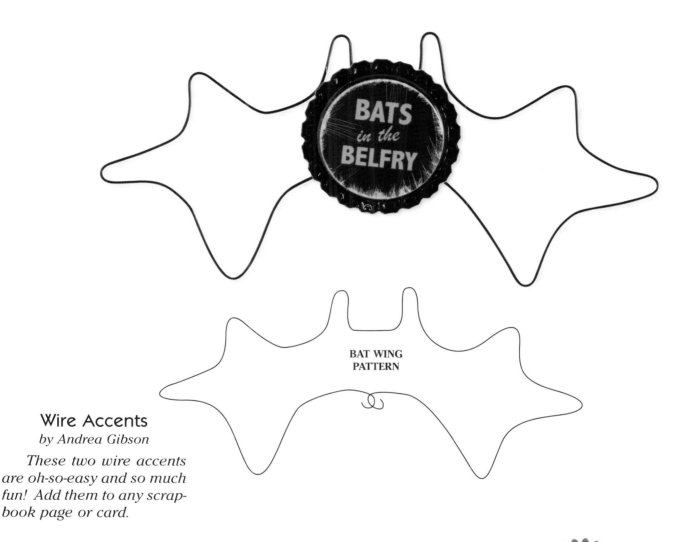

BAT WING PATTERN

Wire Accents
by Andrea Gibson

These two wire accents are oh-so-easy and so much fun! Add them to any scrapbook page or card.

MATERIALS:
Design Originals (Bottle Caps: 1 Black, 1 Orange; #0671 Holiday Sayings Stickers) • *Artistic Wire* (Black 18-20 gauge, Green 24 gauge) • *Tsukineko* StazOn Jet Black ink • Sandpaper • Pliers • Wire cutters • Skewer • Hot glue

INSTRUCTIONS:
Flatten both caps. Punch 3 holes in a row in the Orange cap. • **Bat**: Add the sticker. Scuff lightly with sandpaper. • Cut 16" of Black wire. Shape the wings using the wire diagram. Hot glue the wings to the back of the cap. • **Pumpkin**: Cut 3 Green wires 6" long. Coil around a skewer. Spread the coils. Thread the end through the hole in the cap. Hot glue the wire ends to the back of the cap to secure. • Add the sticker.

PUMPKIN PATTERN

Wire Accents
by Andrea Gibson

ACCENT PATTERN

FLOWER JIG

MATERIALS:
Design Originals (Bottle Caps: 1 Gold, 1 Yellow) • *Artistic Wire* (Copper, Black) • *Tsukineko* StazOn Black ink • *Jacquard* Copper Lumiere • Pliers • Wire cutters • E6000

INSTRUCTIONS:
Flatten the caps. Ink the Yellow cap with Black ink. Paint the Gold cap with Copper. • Punch holes in the caps following the diagram. • **Copper:** Cut 5 Copper wires 6" long. Thread a wire through the cap, across the back and out a hole on the other side, leaving the same length tails on each end. Curl each end into a filigree shape. Repeat for remaining wires. • **Flower:** Cut 16" of Black wire. Thread in and out the holes and shape the inner petals. Twist the ends together at the back to secure. • Cut 30" of Black wire. Thread through the same holes as the inner petal. Shape outer petals. Glue the wire ends to the back of the cap with E6000. Curl 4 Copper spirals. Adhere them to the front of the cap with E6000.

Li'l Squirt
by Diana McMillan

Bright citrus colors attract your eye to this sweet and zesty page.

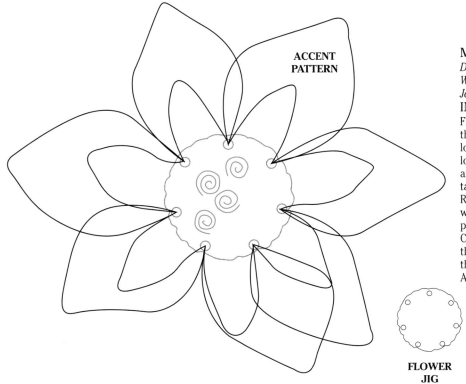

MATERIALS:
Design Originals (Bottle Caps: 4 Orange, 4 Yellow, 4 Green; #0670 Citrus Brights Stickers; #0680 Citrus paper) • *Bazzill* cardstock (Cantaloupe, Peach, Pear, Seafoam) • Clear Micro beads • *ColorBox* Cat's Eye ink (Amber Satin, Olive, Moss Green, Marigold) • Deckle ruler • *JudiKins* Diamond Glaze • *Therm O Web* (Memory Tape Runner, Zots)

INSTRUCTIONS:
Background: Use a deckle to tear the following widths of 12" strips: Cantaloupe 5", Peach 5½", Pear 6", Seafoam 6½". Ink the torn edges. Adhere strips to the Seafoam cardstock. • **Photo**: Adhere the photo to the page with Memory Tape Runner. • **Accents**: Flatten caps. Apply stickers. Adhere caps to the page with Zots. • Adhere beads to the Citrus paper with Glaze. • Adhere wire flower embellishment with Zots. • **Title**: Print title on cardstock.

Flowers and Sunshine with Bottle Caps & Wire

My Daughter... Age 3
by Carrie Edelmann Avery

Bright citrus colors energize this layout with happy memories of non-stop fun.

MATERIALS:

Design Originals (Bottle Caps: Assorted Red, Yellow, Orange; #0680 Citrus paper) • *Karen Foster* decorative Orange papers • *Creative Imaginations* stickers • *My Mind's Eye* die-cut frames • *Wordsworth* clear quote sticker • *Prima* flower • *American Craft* "age 3" stickers • *Magenta* Rust mesh paper • Ribbon • Embossing (Yellow powder, ink pad, heat gun) • Foam tape • Glue dots

INSTRUCTIONS:

Background: Tear about 3" off the left side of the Citrus paper. Lightly tap embossing ink onto the torn edge. Emboss the edge with Yellow. Glue Citrus paper to Orange paper. • **Title**: Flatten the caps. Add letter stickers. Adhere caps in place with foam tape. Adhere quote sticker to 2½" x 5" Orange paper. • Cut an Orange mat 2½" x 4". Adhere the mesh, "3", and "age" stickers. Glue in place. • **Photos**: Adhere photos and die-cut frames to page. Add a flower to the corner of the frame.

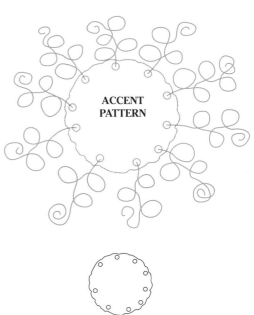

ACCENT PATTERN

ACCENT JIG

All Boy
by Carol Wingert

When your page requires a "scruffy" look to carry an "all boy" theme, swipe it with a bit of sandpaper.

MATERIALS:
Design Originals (Bottle Caps: 1 Orange, 1 Yellow, 1 Aqua , 2 Black; #0673 Typewriter Alphabet Stickers) • *Basic Grey* paper • *Making Memories* staples • Rubber stamps (*PSX, Hero Arts*) • *Clearsnap* Ancient Page ink • Black ribbon • 1" circle punch • Sandpaper • E6000

INSTRUCTIONS:
Background: Sand an 8½" x 8½" piece of striped paper. Adhere the photo in place. • Cut two ⅝" x 9" pieces of stripe paper. Glue them to the page along the top and bottom of the photo. Extend the tabs beyond the edge of the page and staple them in place. • **Accents**: Punch out 4 circles. Stamp "2002" on the Yellow one. Arrange the other 3 circles as shown in the photo. Stamp "all Boy". Glue in place. • Flatten the caps. Lightly sand the stickers and apply to the caps. Adhere caps to the layout with E6000. Punch 2 or more circles as needed to complete the column with the name and glue them in place. • Wrap Black ribbon around bottom of page.

Pocket Watch Cases

Watch Case

Bottle Caps

Flat Metal Rims

Tags

Leaf Spray
Pendant
Frame
Metal Rims
Locket

1" Round Stickers

from *Design Originals*

These versatile 1" images make terrific embellishments. They fit on a variety of shapes.... bottle caps, tags, metal frames, rims, lockets, watch cases, clips, etc.

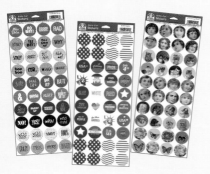

MATERIALS:

Design Originals (Bottle Caps: 6 Silver, 1 Aqua; #0675 Blue Alphabet Stickers) • Cardstock (Blue, Oatmeal, Gray) • *Artistic Wire* 24 gauge (Silver Blue, Non tarnish Silver) • *Magic Scraps* Red seed beads • *Making Memories* Evolution Rub-On letters • Plastic Blue bead • Glitter glue • 1" circle punch • Hot glue • *Therm O Web* (SuperTape, Zots, Foam strips)

INSTRUCTIONS:

Background: Cut a Blue photo mat 9¼" x 11½". Adhere it to the page. • Apply the Rub-On letters to spell out "School" on Blue cardstock. Cut out the word and glue it to the Gray background. • Cut a Blue strip 1½" x 2¾" and adhere it to the page. • **Border**: In each Silver cap, punch 2 holes across from each other. Add Blue Alphabet stickers. Punch out 2 photos and adhere them to 2 caps. • Cut 2 Silver wires 14" long. String the caps and Red beads as shown in the photo. Place the wire borders on the page. Bend the wire ends to the back of the page. Trim as needed and secure with SuperTape. • **Photos**: Cut 4 photos 3⅞" x 5⅛". Cut 4 Oatmeal mats 4⅛" x 5⅜". Adhere mats and photos to the page. • **Fish accent**: Punch holes in the Aqua cap following the diagram. • Cut a 3" Silver Blue wire for the mouth. Cut a 12" Silver Blue wire for the fins and tail. Shape mouth using the diagram and attach to the cap. Secure the wire end with hot glue. • Thread the fin wire through the first top fin hole and out the second hole. Shape the fin using the diagram. Thread the wire through the bottom fin holes and shape. Thread the wire through the tail hole. Add a large blue bead, make a loop and thread the end of the wire back through the bead and into the cap. Shape the tail following the diagram. Secure the wires to the back of the cap with hot glue. • Coil a swirl for the eye. Adhere to the cap with Zots. Add details to the fish with glitter glue. • Cut a Blue mat large enough to support the fish. Cut an Oatmeal mat ¼" larger than the Blue mat. Adhere the Blue mat to the Oatmeal one. Attach the fish to the mat with wire staples. Attach the fish mat to the page with foam tape.

Pool Fish with a Cap and Wire

FISH JIG

Pool School
by Andrea Gibson

Learning to swim is an important step for anyone. Savor the experience with great photos and a page worthy of them. You can almost feel the sunshine and the water when you look at this beautiful page. The fish embellishment is made with wire, a bead, and a cap.

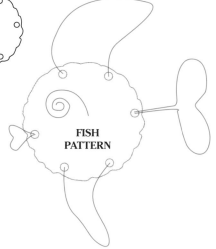

FISH PATTERN

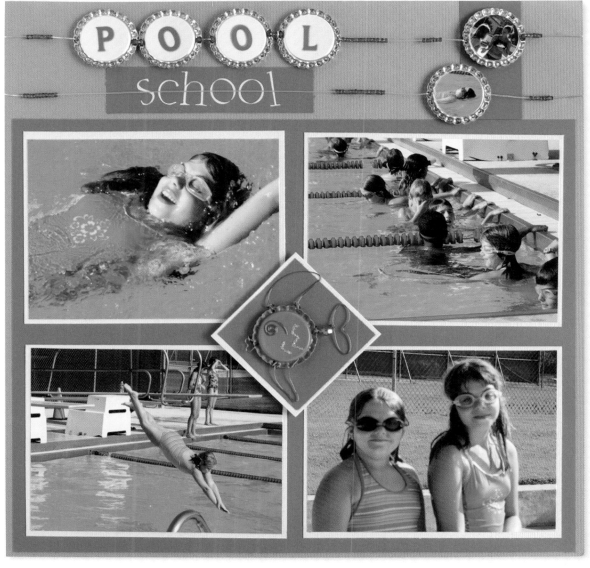

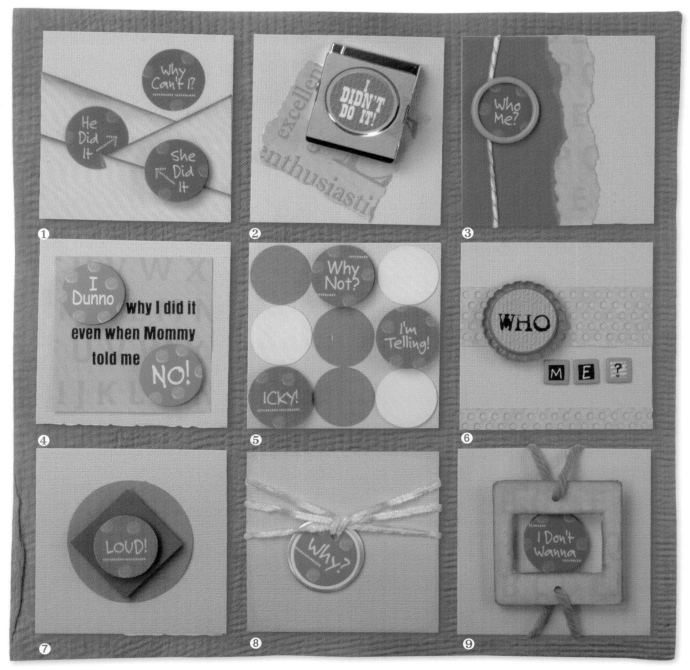

Style with Stickers

1. Cut papers at an angle and ink the edge. Layer papers. Apply stickers. Layer a sticker over another with a foam dot.
2. Tear background paper. Glue a clip. Apply a sticker.
3. Tear papers. Add fibers. Place sticker in a ring brad.
4. Computer print words. Adhere stickers. Layer stickers again with foam dots.
5. Punch out 1" circles. Adhere them to the background. Apply a sticker over the circles with foam tape.
6. Adhere Magic Mesh. Flatten a cap. Apply a sticker. Adhere with foam tape. Add brads with rub-on letters.
7. Cut out a circle and a smaller square. Layer with foam tape. Add a sticker with foam tape.
8. Ink the edges of the background and tag. Apply sticker. Tie 3 strands of fibers to tag. Wrap fibers around edges of cardstock and tape on back.
9. Cover the mount with paper. Ink the edges. Punch a hole in the top and bottom. Adhere sticker to the center with foam tape. Adhere mount with 2 layers of foam tape. Thread yarn through the holes and tie or tape in the back.

MATERIALS:
Design Originals (Papers: #0686 Blue A-Z Word Blocks, #0689 Lime A-Z; Stickers: #1202 Blue Words, #1206 Real Boy; Bottle Caps: 2 Gold, 3 Aqua) • White cardstock • Green Plaid ribbon • Assorted buttons • Markers (Yellow, Green, Turquoise, Black) • Sewing machine • Adhesive

INSTRUCTIONS:
Ink the edges of a 12" White cardstock with Yellow, Green, and Turquoise. • Trim the Lime paper to 11½" square. Sew the Lime paper to the cardstock with a Zig Zag stitch. • Cut a Blue A-Z Word Blocks paper 4¼" x 11½". Ink the edges with Turquoise. Adhere it to the page. • Adhere the photo in place. • Cut 10" of Plaid ribbon. Flatten the bottle caps. Apply the stickers. Adhere the ribbon and caps to the left side of the photo. • Adhere the Blue Words stickers above the photo. • Add journaling with a Black marker. • Cut White cardstock 3¼" x 4½". Write the title with markers. Adhere the title to the page with a Zig Zag stitch. Adhere the buttons in place.

Seeing Circles

Boys will be Boys
by Sherelle Christensen

Here's another way to add drama to a border - flattened bottle caps present words that are "so boy" while rectangular sticker words run across the top of the page like railroad cars expressing more masculine qualities.

Small colored buttons decorate the title of this masculine layout.

Sweet & Small
by Lisa Vollrath

Are you ready for a new photo texture?

It's not just "glossy" or "matte" anymore. Now you can make your photos into a canvas masterpiece. It is really easy to do with an inkjet printer.

You are really going to love the possibilities this technique opens for you. Just make sure that you securely tape the leading edge of fabric to paper so it will run through the printer.

MATERIALS:
Design Originals (#0683 Blue Tag ABCs stickers; Papers: #0728 Baby Bubbles Blue, #0727 Baby Stripes) • White cardstock • *Blumenthal Craft* Photo Fabric • Ribbon (White grosgrain, Blue gingham) • Small safety pins • Inkjet printer • Adhesive • Foam squares

INSTRUCTIONS:
Print photos on fabric following manufacturer's directions. Trim photos and fray edges. • Print text on grosgrain ribbon. • Cut Baby Stripes border 4¾" x 12" and glue it to the bottom of the Baby Bubbles Blue. • Glue printed grosgrain in place. Mount stickers on foam squares. Attach to ribbon with safety pins. Tuck a loop of gingham ribbon under the last sticker and pin in place. Adhere photos with foam squares.

Photos on Fabric

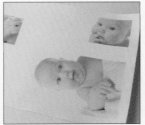

1. Print images on prepared fabric.

2. Trim around images leaving a border.

3. Pull threads to fray the edges.

4. Mount fabric to cardstock.

Computer Printing
on Textiles, Ribbon & Twill

1. Print sheet with guidelines.
2. Apply double stick tape to each line.
3. Stick your ribbons and twill onto the taped guidelines.
4. Tape the leading edge of the ribbons down. Run through the printer.
5. Iron fabric to freezer paper.
6. Image computer printed on canvas.
7. Image computer printed on muslin.
8. Image computer printed on bleached muslin.
9. Apply rub ons to ribbons.

Mona Lisa Smiles
by Lisa Vollrath

This elegant page is quite simple to create. The da Vinci Script background paper and your inkjet printer do most of the work for you.

Accent a fabric photo with a twill ribbon you printed yourself, metal disk frames for beautiful images, and stickers on bottle caps. The result is simply artistic!

MATERIALS:
Design Originals (Papers: #0720 da Vinci Script, #0719 da Vinci Tiles; #1939 Metal Disks; 5 Gold Bottle Caps, #0672 Walnut ABCs stickers) • *Blumenthal Craft* Photo Fabric • Twill tape • *DMC* Pearl Cotton • Inkjet printer • Needle • Rubber mallet • Hammer • Small nail • Adhesive

INSTRUCTIONS:
Print photo on fabric following manufacturer's directions. Trim photo and fray edges. • Print text on twill tape. • Cut 2" circles from da Vinci Tiles paper and adhere the images to the centers of the metal disks. • Adhere the photo, twill tape and disks in place. Flatten 5 bottle caps and punch a hole in each rim. Stitch caps to twill, knotting and trimming end. Apply stickers to the caps.

Paris - Forever and Always
by Lisa Vollrath

For those of you who love collage, the clipboard is a most versatile canvas. You can alter it, display it, and then when you are ready for a new project, take it apart and make something different.

This clipboard uses plexiglass to protect a vintage postcard. It provides a nice way for the novice to practice collage, and will inspire the experienced artist to look at clipboards with new eyes.

MATERIALS:
Design Originals (#1854 Silver Bottle Cap; Papers: #0719 da Vinci Tiles, #0720 da Vinci Script; #1212 Art Elements stickers) • Small clipboard • Amber sheer ribbon • Black Rub-On • Black typewriter key letters • Eiffel Tower postcard • 4" x 6" plexiglass sheet • *ColorBox* Amber Clay Chalk inkpad • E6000 • Glue stick

INSTRUCTIONS:
Adhere the da Vinci Script paper to the front of the clipboard. Age the edges with Amber Clay. Cut a piece of da Vinci Tiles paper, 3 squares wide by 4 squares high. Center it under the clip and glue it to the clipboard. • Position the postcard and plexiglass under the clip. If desired, glue the postcard in place. Use typewriter letters to write "Paris" on the plexiglass. • Apply Rub-On text to the sheer ribbon. Wrap the ribbon around the bottom of the clipboard diagonally as shown, wrapping around the back of clipboard to glue in place. • Apply a sticker to a flattened Silver bottle cap. Adhere the cap to the clipboard. • Tie a bow around the clip and trim ribbon tails to desired length.